Electric Sarcasm

Dimitra Ioannou

This is the description of critical darkness that includes

                        a

                        tarot

                        deck,

                        golden

                        visas,

                        plastic

                        referendums,

                        defaulting

                        democracies,

                        all on

                        the same

                        floor,

                        hollow

                        above

                        below

                        solid.

as if the 21st century is a durational performance
all that is slipping out of our mouths and then retracting
archival materials, payment histories, exuberance
almost €100 billion and dark imaginings

Unfavourable terms are diffused across the palate. That's why the echo in the neo/colonies is an elegy. Is "elegy" a new word for something that happens? Are elegies part of the rulers' indestructible verbal machine? Do they reflect the rulers' historical present, their bowls full of delectable cranberries, blanched almonds, and nuts, their gold and silver-tone stone chokers, £645 each? No. I never had a money line on my palm.

These are some of the collectable coins that I use for the monthly installments of my credit card. They are so shiny that the clerks keep asking me where did I find them, and I say they are medieval, my only inheritance.

Is that true? So true is it that the bankers keep tracking me. Is that true? So true is it that I turned my real name into a pseudonym. Is that true? So true is it that my pseudonym became my signature. Is that true? So true is it that my signature represents nothing more than Gothic darkness, a fantasy.

"Durational," as in the phrases "durational transition," "durational projection," "durational set-up."

And the terms feel like imitations verités, or labyrinthine game descriptions. And pseudonyms are worshipped for their supposed magical powers. So elegies are about coins that are counterfeited on the way to the market, or about absorbance. And the black market is surrounded by continuously rolling cameras so elegies stop themselves. And the performance is about sensors, shelters, and the frantic movement of cardholders. And their fantasies feel like bandaging techniques.

My clothes are made of intricately sewn elegies and elegies can be fireworks, exclamations, a return of the same, ordinary events, and virtual realms.

I take the bus that runs along the Avenue of the Banker, the speculator of rise and fall, nowadays a name without bank. The name of my stop is Tax // Phoros //

> phoreas
>
> // the
>
> agent,
>
> bearer,
>
> or producer
>
> of a
>
> specified
>
> thing
>
> // le néant
>
> // an obscene
>
> term
>
> // a bidder
>
> and a bird

They say that those who learn their own λanguage can only negotiate. My terms are a magic trick from the Old French taxer, from the Latin taxare "to censure, charge, compute', perhaps from Greek tassein, to "fix" what it is and what its limits are, what it is like, the opposite of who I am.

тax   тax   тax me
тax me at the Golden gate to Europe
while I link up to a whole, the whole model

тaxation as indefinite time in one's life
the vulgar тax
hot flashes four hours south

Am I not a hard-line supplicant? Don't debtors supplicate to be made archivists?

тax   тax   тax me   my senses are transfixed by the coppered claws of a hawk
тax the receptors   тax the mechanics   тax me

Am I going to make the symbol freeze? Will they tarnish? Am I going to transform the acute pain, collective traumas, false conclusions, straining desires, and a number of boundaries into a historical distance? Will that be a history of no having? Is "history" the wrong word for something that is experienced as "if"?

ᴛax me while I store suspicious phone numbers under the names of
*Le Capitalisme 1, Le Capitalisme 2, Le Capitalisme 3, Le
   Capitalisme 4,*
Encore le Capitalisme, or *Est-ce bien le Capitalisme?*

ᴛax me in a way that is different each time, retrospectively

as if my mobile phone is a contemporary re-creation
as if a list of capitalistic pseudo-contacts doesn't imply a set of
   rules
as if the names in French exoticize the provenance and the
   attempts
as if my economic body is not standard thus exploitable

is the tax not like this   levied on pasturage slaughtering,
the use of basic materials, coherence, or the raising of pigs

ᴛax post-privacy postures   ᴛax my irrational digits

as if an unanswered call is part of a process-oriented work
as if refusal always has to be restructured
as if I can use *l'annuaire du capitalisme* to collect behavioral
   data
as if the work becomes gargantuan and disruptive

ᴛax   ᴛax   ᴛax me

Remember language in the times of expansion, the way glimmers merged with oracles, the arteries of mythology, bodies crawling across the stock markets, countless projections.

As if in economic miracles meaning imitates magic. As if only a miracle could save the stock market. As if national elections can result in miracles, and voters can come out ahead of the system because miracles happen.

I used to eat credit card food, the milk of agreements. Give me some. Give me more than that. We can all become masters of distraction.

Is that a verbal or post-verbal offer? Are we saving History for later because today we are being constantly rewarded? Are we talking smoothly? Are we going to have endless conversations about cutlery, the porcelain ambition, rococo swallowing, wearable *objets d'art*, the right attitude, order over intuition? Are we going to focus on textures in order to make meaning?

Meaning, the furry. Meaning, brimming with receipts, and disproportional gifts. Meaning, by the pool in the woods. Meaning, as one of the laws for the protection of property. Meaning, the bubbly.

Give me consolation organic, the highest available light reduction, hyper-fast, hyper-optic fibres, the caring lavender, foundation transcendent, more time, myths of the right now, affection vinyl.

As they slowly press the debts to our wrists, we are not allowed withdrawal.

Is that the incoming present tense, the central present tense, the centralistic present tense   OR   we don't know why we tell that present tense but we tell it regardless? Is that the present tense's greatest asset?

Is that the most spreading, the most inexhaustible present tense   OR   the most frequent from anywhere else present tense?

Is that the present tense that is screaming in my face, the present tense that is aggressively pushing me into a smaller and smaller area   OR   the non present tense?

Is that the present tense that moves back and forth between impasses, the dramatically weakened present tense   OR   the present tense that knew details once but now forgets?

Is that the present tense of the identical ones   OR   are they being reduced in that present tense? Is that the annihilating   OR   the annihilated present tense?

Is that the present tense in the first person, the present tense that does not recognise any other present tense   OR   the subsequent present tense?

Is that the present tense of savers   OR   the present tense of fools, the present tense of wombs, the present tense that is reborn as a hashtag poem that includes the hashtags *chimaera* and *emptythreat*?

I would be shouting *enough* if I wasn't shouting *now*, because the now is an attribute, my attribute, the skin membrane, the chiroptera and the bones of the bat that went down the chimney, my spare fact, the glossary of falling.

I would be shouting *catch it* if I wasn't shouting *now*, because the now caught us by surprise, it speaks an intractable omen, so interwoven with mathematics that it is hard to even appropriate it.

I would be shouting *there* if I wasn't shouting *now*, because the now is the technology of fortune I am working on, it demands new meanings, on the dark side of the horizon which is not really a horizon rather a dividing line of bodies.

I would be shouting *countless* if I wasn't shouting *now*, because the now is my matter, my materiality, what I recognise in others and what the others recognise in me, my animal thinking, my camóuflage tongue in a perpetual consumption.

I would be shouting *exhausted* if I wasn't shouting *now*, because the now is in my power, it always was, how could it not be otherwise, how could I not have been aware of?

I would be shouting *zophos* if I wasn't shouting *now*, because the now starts with a deficit, and ends with a question mark, it calls up the senseless calculations I made hurriedly while trying to distinguish tyche from wrong.

I would be shouting *syn* if I wasn't shouting *now*, because the now records and codifies every single move, and tracks the planners' input, the planners of input, their plans renounced and revoked.

By 2015, I would shout OXI along with 61,30 percent of voters. For many that anti-austerity vote would have entailed some kind of independence, or a strategy of survival. For others it was rather an attempt to give debt a λanguage.

It would have sprung from what the economic planners called the "bottomless pit."

Oh, the bottomless pit that symbolises a country and the vagina, abandonment and hell, that unreliable negotiator. So much contempt for those who live in the bottomless pit that is a country on the periphery of a centre. So many blows, vindictive and violent gestures. Their bodies are whirling along with wrappers, cartons, and bags unable to repair the walls, or set ablaze the headquarters. They watch their civic matter in rot or in rage, neglected, beaten, ridiculed, celebrated, in solidarity or in conflict, shamed or dispossessed, silenced, dancing, claiming, daring. They are their own spectacle. The spectacle's meaning is either accelerated or decelerated, depending on pension cuts, riot squads, smoke from wildfires, bankruptcy courts, suicides, femicides, closures. Their movements look awkward, and mostly sketch meanings, like "a pit is something that belongs to a Union," or "in bottomless pits there are no marked exits." There is no architecture without action, no architecture without events, no architecture without program. By extension there is no architecture without violence. "Violence" is a metaphor for the intensity of a relationship between individuals and their surrounding spaces. \ Bernard Tschumi / What keeps them up most nights is the violence of their fantasies of plenitude.

as if they are replicas of themselves, and are given context
as if there won't be enough time although there will
as if they are going to be confused forever
as if time in debt is degraded

Oh, the finance capital, so ruthlessly sacred and profane, it hurts the eyes and the ears of those it targets. They cannot distinguish the periphery from the deadlock, the State from the Union, the Union from the banks. Their actions seem meaningless, their movements are out of sync, and the entire spectacle looks so poor that it feels entirely imagined. Meaningless! Can you imagine? What kind of mechanism would that be? Are they not dancers?

In darkness, in occupation, in rugs, in the 1970s and in the 2020s, the dancing body is curled up, on the back, on the floor, and is trying to get up slowly, repeatedly. It loses its balance and footing, and collapses to the ground over and over again. Get up from the floor, my body, my scars, my lungs and poisoned tissues, my deterioration. You are anathema to the planners who manage the common land.

I want to make up for the ellipsis, and feed my own dreams, memories, and desires into the movement \ Masaki Iwana /, this is all I want to do now, and dance.

What are they dancing? Are they rotating in instances hypnotic like "thickness," "intertia blatant" or "the positive list of reimbursed medicines"? Does she rise up to express the "patchwork walls in a room," and "words without audience"? Is his body danced by "the eerie"? Do her ribs start to contract upon the realisation that she "can't even afford the passport"? Are they jumping in "debt denial"? Does she stay straight while drawing from her strongest intuition, "I am about to be excluded"? Do they roll on the floor as "fabrics," "meltdown," and "mere legumes"? Do I perform "the work of one night"? Are they dancing the spectacle of austerity? Does she bow like "insomnia in winter"?

Meaning, as they go under. Meaning, stripped from its aim. Meaning, in the space underneath. Meaning, from Point Zero. Meaning, for recovering the base body. Meaning, in micro-movements. Meaning, undergoing combustion. Meaning, as damaged goods. Meaning, moment chaotic. Meaning, craving.

Somewhere between stagnation and unrest, we become visible thus electric.

There are four major banks in the country, and they are valued more than are 10 million people. They are considered sacred by the country's rulers, for otherwise finance (both originating in that country and brought in from outside) will leave the country and move elsewhere, reducing it to illiquidity and disrupting its economy \ Prabhat Patnaik /, who act as arbitrarily as is necessary to protect them.

It is April, and it is July, it is the salmon pink, and the greedy green, the colours of salad, in 2010 and 2015. The international lenders are staying at the oldest chain hotel in town. The cultural distinctiveness of the elites in the informational society is to create a lifestyle and to design spatial forms aimed at unifying the symbolic environment of the elite around the world, thus superseding the historical specificity of each locale. \ Manuel Castell / Here the meaning is marbled and visibly armed. No doubt about that. It is the front aspect of the ellipsis. Strategically speaking.

There is a shortage of medical staff, and equipment, gloves, catheters, spoons, forks, and cleaning tissues. *Bring your own staff. Sheets might be needed too.* It is late, and it is deteriorating, and yet the hotel remains an anchor of safety for the elite staff, so it makes one wonder if their economic programs are designed for preventing them from being infected. There is a major difference between a luxury hotel and a public hospital. The former is managerial, the later is expendable. Besides being diametrically opposed, one of them is leaning towards the ephemeral. Hygiene becomes primordial.

It is leathered, and it is sparkly, the way binaries, limits and detours make sense to the elite lenders. During the negotiations, they say that they are not going to accept a package of small measures, criticise the negotiating style of the other party as "insulting" and "obstructive," and declare that promises no longer suffice. Technical discussions resume in the outskirts. The party that needs a very large amount of money has to sign something to be remembered. In order to make sure it will comply with the terms of the rescue, the elite lenders warn about the dangers of the non space, which in this case is the country outside the centre and the periphery altogether, the worst-case scenario for imports.

It is small, and it is tricky, so objectively untrue, and yet the "bottomless pit" is one of their best acquisitions. Sovereignty buying is the ultimate deal. The pit is the medium. The money goes back with high interest to the lenders. That, basically, is a defect.

It is January, and it is February, a birthday and a burial, and I stand where no writing can be done. There is a shortage of words that goes along with the shortage of cash. For instance, I have three euros for the rest of the month, or year, and I cannot even use three words to describe the ellipsis. So I listen to what the others have to say. What they relay to me is a false account of what I experience, and I believe them. It is their story, and it sounds normal. The facts are generic, the food is generic, the conditions, the apartments, and the emotions too. Everything is as banal as the clothes we are wearing.

My private distress. Your private distress. Theirs.

This is where the metaphor of the bottomless pit actually fits. All of our stories disappear into its depths. They are so many. They are unbearable. They lose their meaning. Is it not because the whole situation is too costly, too deadlocked, too unpaid, too unfair, too inside, and sticky, too senior, and sick, too underpaid, too financial to be confronted?

Unlock the knees. Hell is submerged by dangerous rhetoric. It threatens a pit to remain forever bottomless, boasts about its expertise in restructuring, and announces the surveillance cycle. Language casts sheaves of reality upon the social body, stamping it and violently shaping it. \ Monique Wittig / Is the language we are exposed to exposed to us?

There are no bearers of gifts to beware of, we have no (real) income, we are out of their reach. Are we becoming anonymous? And if so, what kind of anonymity is that? What is it not leaking? Massively?

Tax reverberations, and strict sadness

I think of threads that have been entangled in crashed time and crashed energy, the present's compost, what became available and what was feared most, details or elements of error that form patterns, which some name "nonobjective," "asymmetrical," or "interlocking," and others "redness," or "collapsing."

One may discern in the patterns the excess of agony, the rage against avatars, avatars in the firmament, constant intrusion, heated metal doors and poorly forged data, the black spots on the mirror, a water heater that was broken for two years, clothes that were bought on the streets for 1 to 5 euros, the value revisited, hesitations adamant, the irreconcilable and the pragmatic, poverty's code   OR   the present tense that becomes a Chimaera of the times.

Was there a reason for this? No desire at all. I call that mass *anathema*, the body that opposes and retorts: *Are we together in the breeze abyss? Without form.*

#this is the place of a hashtag poem
#about deceleration, moonbows, and cats,
#about the white ring around the moon
#and the bright δίοδος (passage) that links
#the Athenian Zone with the universe
#around 21:00,
#about the dance as public protest
#and Vrisoules, the Little Fountains, the she activists who sing,
#FarewellLittleFountainsMountainsAndRidges,
#against the drilling of oil and gas in Epirus,
#about what we still love and cherish
#against the false narratives of economic growth
#that won't bring the crisis to an end

#my favourite elegy is about the red hibiscus that died in my place

In the dream, the strike was a chain of bubbles. Political slogans rang out, but the night was handmade, and our deeds were nebulous. The slogans demanded the impossible, so they did not have the power to irk either the government or its creditors. The so called vagina-abandonment-cum-hell echoed a subterranean whisper, cries, or smoke from burnt grass.

In the dream, in November, in the Athenian Zone, in 2019, in the police state, Silence is Λanguage in disguise, a trail on the streets, somewhere near, looking for tools, topic bubbles, the counter-genealogy of words. It drifts around until it finds the empty premises of a small business that imported lingerie from China and went bankrupt. They are marbled and cold, but later on vibrate the energy of slam poetry, so they become hot and fleshy.

In the novel, in the 13th century, in the Roman de Silence, in the law, in the family, the girl is brought up as a boy so that he may be able to inherit her parents. She was sworn to silence so that is his name. Until the age of twelve she thinks he is a boy, and when duties and customs become oppressive, or confusing, Scilenscius or Scilencia darken their skin with an herb, and run away with two minstrels. They change class and race, and take the name of Malduit. Mal*con*duit? Duit, an old coin of the Netherlands and Dutch controlled territories. Mal. duit, money in general in Malaysian slang.

Dreams of ciphers, old anti-colonial proverbs, copper coins. Replaced each letter of the Greek alphabet with a symbol, and read from my diaries in *The Closet* reading series. My voice resonated from deep in Scilenscia's throat. She had changed that *-us* into *-a* and returned to the homeland to give me four duit back.

I need liquidity. I need to copy the structure of certain plant leaves. And I need to say more than I am capable.

I would perform a poetic ritual in the lobby, and in the toilets of the international hotel that usually accommodates the Troika staff. I would watch the officials, and think of a word to express my anger. I would go to the bathroom and spell it on my naked body, or the wall. In another ritual, I would print photos of their faces, and write about them.

These rituals were suggested by CA Conrad during his workshop in Athens, in September 2017. They would make my λanguage flow. I would transform the orders of doing and undoing into a text which cannot immediately be given one single correct meaning by its reader. \ Michèle Le Doeuff / That atopia would provoke the abolition of all meaning which is also the abolition of temporality. \ Kathy Acker / I would replace words mechanically and make sentences impossible in real life \ Hiromi Ito / in order to maltreat the meaning of the Growth Strategy. Even if the language we think of as critical can easily "lend itself" to the very techniques of governance we critique \ Sara Ahmed /, the abolition of temporality would free the text from all governance. In hierarchical terms, that would be a sub-text, the ghost behind their definitions. \ Alice Notley /

My atopia, my non topos, and non text, demand redemption and recompense.

How to Conceive a Troika

Ah, troika, troika, swift as a bird, who was it first invented you?
—Nikolai Gogol.

The troika is a traditional Russian sleigh or carriage drawn by three horses harnessed abreast. In the context of the European crisis, the Troika includes three institutions. The Troika is conceptual, and dramatic.

Troika and Country are inextricable. The troika was developed around the 17th to 18th century as a method of quickly crossing Russia's lengthy and hazardous roads. The Troika acted for the first time in 2010, in Greece. Then, isn't Troika epic?

The main character in Nikolai Gogol's novel, *Dead Souls* (1842), goes across Russia in a troika to buy the dead souls of various landowners. In Tsarist Russia the ownership of serfs is described as owning "souls." The owners of souls were taxed on their payroll of serfs, which included those who had died between tax-assessments. What is the Troika dragging? Where to?

If the Troika's ambition is to become speed, then the political establishment's ambition is to exceed the social, thus becoming the seller of souls, and common land. Meaning, if need will adopt. Meaning, to feed into the system. Meaning, as facilitation, implementation, regulations, billion, absorption. Meaning, as the negative list of reimbursed medicines. Meaning, denied. When people are tired of whirling, they stain with blood the Memorandums of Understanding.

From 2010 to 2014, from Athens' wastewater treatment plant, an international team of researchers collected and analysed samples, and found that the use of antipsychotics, benzodiazepines, and antidepressants has skyrocketed since the first bailout plan took effect in 2010.

We shouldn't waste so much time. The extension is only for four months and the clock is ticking. In the bailout series, the Troika is the guarantor of time, and the Country the time waster. C'est la Fin, the Finance, the seller of monetised time and buyer of construction sites where that time will be shaped accordingly, from *finer* "make an end, settle a debt," which later had the sense of taxation, and revenue, and now represents the global financial market that exploits all resources and accelerates the end of species. The future is colonized, packaged, and sold as bets on future valuation, and as options between various future scenarios. \ Manuell Castell / To be occupied is to be fictionally generated.

Ah, Troika, Troika, lethal as finance, you sacrifice easily, but you have such a limited imagination. There won't be any future, you are actually killing it. No one will carry out your plans for too long, not even your loyal servants. Stupid Troika, you are nothing more than fear.

echo:

"

This

is not

    the night of recession

but

    the night of jaybirds.

They carry

    under their tongue

the cost

    of what

we are deemed

    to be missing

"

Time is delayed, overripe, another crisis in the relation between the society and the State, the Centre and the Periphery, the banks and their customers, the banks and the society, the society in the Centre and the society in the Periphery, between the States of the Centre, or else a palimpsest that few can afford to read anymore, let alone sustain. The gangrenous parts of the Centre are thrown into the "bottomless pit," and we eat them. It was infested anyway.

Tax the mother city that doesn't last, or lasts for too long

Tax my tone   Tax the analogy that becomes richer

As we lose our economic rights and plunge into poverty, we become contemporaries thus atopians. As if these molecules that amass dystopia, further and continually, are out of context, and occupy a non topos, the only place that nowadays we can actually have. That is an atopima, another word in Greek for describing the breeze abyss, movements from below, the fading normal. Atopia is not a model; instead it is a potential access to a different positive perspective on our present world. \ Yves Millet /

Tax the euphemism, *Financial Stability Fund*
Tax the hyperbole, *So I say to you*

When the mother company goes bankrupt, the managers flee, and an entire factory is standing idle, instead of accepting the facts, and survive on unemployment benefits, one might attempt an atopima. In Thessaloniki, since 2013, a 25,000-square-foot factory has been occupied by 23 of its former workers. They are their fifties, and the whole neighbourhood supported them when they decided to seize the means of production as a "recompense" for due wages. They now produce ecological cleaning products, and vegetable oil soaps by popular demand.

#this is the place of a hashtag poem
#about the use of white vinegar in cleaning solutions
#and *Afissolini*, a glue for adhering posters to walls,
#about the force of circumstance and local centuries
#that do not comply with the Text Centres

#when swifts and swallows are flown off course by heavy winds,
#and land in the streets, they bring their time with them

Changes depend on mirrors, when all around are exchange privileges. In the land of mirrors you are

>
> my
>
> endorphin
>
> release,
>
> my
>
> ecstatic
>
> moonbow,
>
> my
>
> Haemostatic
>
> Cherry Pink,
>
> my
>
> Haemostatic
>
> Indigo,
>
> a key to a code,
>
> my λanguage,
>
> kleidouchos
>
> (the key-bearer),
>
> my present tense.

Atopima 1

Spend the mornings working on a λanguage that restore pheasants. "Sentimental Treasures" is the title on the cover of the vintage photo album. Focus on the roast pheasant's taste. Roast, pheasant and taste depend on the mother tongue which is neither yours nor theirs. Type the words *sentimental, expensive, diversion*. They say nothing about you. Become the waste that is the meal.

Atopima 2

Ignore language of strong contrasts and deep shadows. Wrap the abyss around it like a shawl. This is your bargaining power. No one can see through it, only you.

Atopima 3

In times of communiques and planning, read the Chimaera theory. Define the "theory" between 3-4 h in the morning for four consecutive nights. Scrawl on yourself LOVE INDOLENCE. Release your definitions into the breeze. Chimaera is the breeze. Take on its punctuation; if there is one; if one can wait.

Atopima 4

The Glossary of Austerity is a deviate of the Lush Glossary. Talk to yourself as if your face does not match predictions. Try to make that in the company of others. There might be no answer, but there will be a solution. Atopima betrays plans.

Atopima 5

The slogan behind the DJ set reads, BEWARE OUR IDLE MASTERS. Take a screenshot of the wall, print it, make a copy, then copy its copy until *poverty* becomes a word beyond recognition. Dance a proto-dance. Shortly before 9am on a Monday, tweet "the dance routine."

Atopima 6

By dusk, listen to the supplicant. Her demand is huge: *Will you buy me some time? You always did that.* Offer her what she doubts the most. As you are running out of money, ask her, *Don't you need money*? Even if you don't realise your own words, you feed time with concrete λanguage.

Atopima 7

I speak your name, the name that you don't speak. One day you ask what is the point of remembering the family bankruptcy, or the bad things in general. We both started working at a young age. That is your legacy, our intelligence, the tongue, truth, and margins that we should not have sold to anyone, especially not to our distractors. Now speak my name, as if I were not your double.

Atopima 8

Read a page from a text you love because it was not written for you. Gaze into that page as if it were a pit. A pit is a part of the floor of a stock exchange in which a particular stock or commodity is traded, and hell. Whenever you feel like it, scream: *Throw stocks and bonds over your heads, and futures will be born.* Tax the political industry as madness from within.

Atopima 9

Curse warnings to be reduced to pieces. Use dark ecologist λanguage. Put your palms on warning letters, so as to superimpose your fingerprints on the paper. That is a way for the mu / 無 to pervade hazards. While listening to abyss pop, or post-lyric folklore rhythms, tear up the warning letters.

Atopima 10

When feeling tired of expiry dates, complaints, and upheavals, watch the chamomile sect invading the green. That could be on the outside of the #PagodaOfLostPleasures. The goddess and the god is you. Bring in what is gradually taken out of history. Lick my bones. Become a flower thief.

If pathogens modify terms, if omens get out of hand, if debtors gossip, is it not because conditions are corruptible like any reflection, or sequence? I might not tell anyone. Who would you, today, call the bearer?

References

Kathy Acker, "My Death, My Life by Pier Paolo Pasolini," 1983; published in *Blood and Guts in High School*, Picador, 1984.

Sara Ahmed, "Declarations of Whiteness: The Non-Performativity of Anti-Racism," 2004. http://www.borderlands.net.au/vol3no2_2004/ahmed_declarations.htm

Manuell Castell, "The Information Age: Economy, Society and Culture," John Wiley & Sons, second edition, 2010.

Michèle Le Doeuff, *The Philosophical Imaginary*, Stanford University Press, 1989.

Hiromi Ito, *Killing Kanoko*, Action Books, 2009.

Masaki Iwana, http://www.iwanabutoh.com/butoh.php

Yves Millet, "Atopia & Aesthetics. A Modal Perspective," *Contemporary Aesthetics* (CA), Volume 11, 2013. https://quod.lib.umich.edu/c/ca/7523862.0011.017/--atopia-amp-aesthetics-a-modal-perspective?rgn=main;view=fulltext

Alice Notley, *In the Pines*, Penguin Books, 2007.

Prabhat Patnaik, "Notes on Contemporary Imperialism," 2010. https://mronline.org/2010/12/20/notes-on-contemporary-imperialism/

"Interview: Prabhat Patnaik on Contemporary Capitalism and the Shape It Takes in India" https://thewire.in/economy/prabhat-patnaik-interview-capitalism

Eric Toussaint, "Banks are responsible for the crisis in Greece," 2017. www.cadtm.org/Banks-are-responsible-for-the

Bernard Tschumi, "Violence of Architecture," *Artforum*, December 1981.

Darren J. Lim, Michalis Moutselos & Michael McKenna, "Puzzled out? The unsurprising outcomes of the Greek bailout negotiations," 2018. www.tandfonline.com/doi/full/10.1080/13501763.2018.1450890.

Monique Wittig, *The Straight Mind And Other Essays*, Beacon Press, 1992.

Glossary

Anathema (ανάθεμα): in common usage, something or someone that is detested or shunned.

Atopema (atópima): atopia, impertinence, absurdity, paradox

Ellipsis (έλλειψη): scarcity, shortage.

mu (無): nothing, zero, void.

Syn is the Greek word for plus.

Zophos (ζόφος): murky, appalling gloom, referring to darkness so dense and foreboding it is "felt"; (figuratively) apocalyptic, gloomy darkness associated with the nether world (BAGD) bringing its indescribable despair (incredible gloom).

Acknowledgments

The poem that starts with the line "as if the 21st century is a durational performance" was first published in *Splinter* magazine, Issue No 5: February 2019

Thanks to Anna Moschovakis; Antonis Katsouris; Olga Ioannou; Anna Varoufaki; Kate Skoura.

Electric Sarcasm
Copyright © Dimitra Ioannou, 2020

2020 Pamphlet Series
ISBN 978-1-946433-51-0
First Edition, First Printing
Edition of 1,000

Ugly Duckling Presse
The Old American Can Factory
232 Third Street, #E-303
Brooklyn, NY 11215
uglyducklingpresse.org

Distributed in the USA by SPD/Small Press Distribution
Distributed in the UK by Inpress Books

Series design by chuck kuan and Sarah Lawson
Typeset by Don't Look Now!
Type is New Century Schoolbook
Cover paper and flyleaf from French Paper Co.
Printed offset and bound at McNaughton & Gunn
Flyleaf printed letterpress at Ugly Duckling Presse

This publication is made possible, in part, by support from the New York State Council on the Arts, a state agency. This project is supported by the Robert Rauschenberg Foundation.

 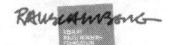

This pamphlet is part of UDP's 2020 Pamphlet Series: twenty commissioned essays on poetics, translation, performance, collective work, pedagogy, and small press publishing. The authors are listed below; their pamphlets are available for individual purchase and as a subscription (uglyducklingpresse.org/subscribe). Each offers a different approach to the pamphlet as a form of working in the present, an engagement at once sustained and ephemeral.

Mirene Arsanios
~~Omar Berrada~~*
Sergio Chejfec
Don Mee Choi
Kunci Study Forum & Collective
Iris Cushing
Simon Cutts
Nicole Cecilia Delgado
Adjua Gargi Nzinga Greaves
Dimitra Ioannou

Sibyl Kempson
Claudia La Rocco
Aditi Machado
Chantal Maillard
Tinashe Mushakavanhu
Sawako Nakayasu
Tammy Nguyen
Aleksandr Skidan
Steven Zultanski
Magdalena Zurawski

*Nadine George-Graves & Okwui Okpokwasili

To win a subscription, write to office@uglyducklingpresse.org with your solution to the following puzzle: Using only 6 straight lines, divide the circle on the back cover so that each number is in its own section, without any overlap between numbers.